D0231616

Country
Wit

summersdale

COUNTRY WIT

Summersdale Publishers Ltd
46 West Street
Chichester
West Sussex
PO19 1RP
UK

www.summersdale.com

Printed and bound in Great Britain

ISBN: 978-1-84024-704-6

Disclaimer
Every effort has been made to attribute the quotations in this collection to the correct source. Should there be any omissions or errors in this respect we apologise and shall be pleased to make the appropriate acknowledgements in any future editions.

Country Wit

Aubrey Malone

Contents

Editor's Note

The countryside is often hailed as 'the green and pleasant land', but on a grey day in February it can be cold, soggy and decidedly miserable. Weather permitting, rural retreats can be paradise, but when you're soaked to the skin on a foggy mountainside and the sun, or whatever you can see of it, is setting, maybe a small part of you regrets you didn't instead opt for the five-star hotel in London with the spa, the penthouse and the digital TV.

Country folk may appear to be a different breed from their town cousins, with their oft outmoded hunter-gatherer leisure pursuits, morris dancing and worship of four-legged friends, but in these pages you'll find some witticisms to engage you regarding the bittersweet delights of lives lived far from bright neon lights or the steady drone of traffic.

The perspective isn't dewy-eyed or rose-tinted. In fact, it's often the city dweller that has an overly romantic attitude to the country, because they only see it in its radiant glory. In these pages we dodge the cowpats, cross pastures green and get both sides of the divide: for better and/or worse.

DOWN ON THE FARM

Serendipity means
searching for a needle
in a haystack and
instead finding a
farmer's daughter.

Hermann Bondi

There's something
about a farm that
gets you... particularly
if the wind's in the
wrong direction.

Janet Rogers

Dance with the girl that
has the looks, but marry the
one who has the farm.

Proverb

In the bad old days, there were
three easy ways of losing money
– racing being the quickest,
women the pleasantest and
farming the most certain.

William Amherst

The farmer allows walkers across the field for free, but the bull charges.

Sign on an Irish gate

Physically there's nothing to distinguish human society from the farmyard except that children are more troublesome and costly than chickens.

George Bernard Shaw

The only men who can lose money
every year, live well, educate their
children and die rich are farmers.

Hal Roach

A good farmer is nothing
more nor less than a handy
man with a sense of humus.

E. B. White

Money is like manure, of very little use except it be spread.

Francis Bacon

You got to have smelt a lot of mule manure before you can sing like a hillbilly.

Hank Williams

Only he can
understand what
a farm is, what a
country is, who shall
have sacrificed part
of himself to his farm
or country, fought
to save it, struggled
to make it beautiful.
Only then will the
love of farm or
country fill his heart.

Antoine de Saint-Exupéry

A NATION OF
CAT LOVERS

We've got a cat called
Ben Hur. We called it
Ben till it had kittens.

Sally Poplin

Men are better
than cats because
they only pee on
loo carpets.

Jo Brand

They put on the exact same
look when they see a moth
or an axe murderer.

Paula Poundstone on the problem with cats

Cats are smarter than dogs. You
can't get eight of them to pull a
sledge through snow, for instance.

Jeff Valdez

A dog is a man's best friend.
A cat is a cat's best friend.

Robert Vogel

Home Wanted for Feline: Willing
to do Light Mousework.

Newspaper ad

———•———

I was informed the training procedure
with cats was difficult. It's not.
Mine had me trained in two days.

Bill Dana

———•———

A cat isn't fussy, just as long as
you remember he likes his milk in the
shallow rose-patterned saucer and
his fish on the blue plate, from which
he will take it and eat it off the floor.

Arthur Bridges

My cat is very intelligent. I asked her what two minus two was and she said nothing.

Brian Johnston

When my cats aren't happy, I'm not happy. Not because I care about their mood but because I know they're just sitting there thinking up ways to get even.

Percy Bysshe Shelley

NEIGHSAYERS

There are two things
you should avoid
approaching from
the rear: restaurants
and horses.

Evelyn Waugh

I prefer a bike to a horse. The brakes are more easily checked.

Lambert Jeffries

Love and marriage go together like a horse and carnage.

Bob Monkhouse

Love and marriage may go
together like a horse and carriage,
but a horse and carriage is
usually followed by manure.

Suzanne Tumy

There are two important
rules in horse-riding. The first
is to mount the horse. The
second is to stay mounted.

John Mortimer

It's nonsense expecting Prince Charming to come along on his beautiful white horse – you're better off keeping the horse instead.

Julie Newmar

A horse is dangerous at both ends and uncomfortable in the middle.

Ian Fleming

For every set of horseshoes
people use for luck, somewhere out
there there's a barefoot horse.

Allan Sherman

Princess Anne looks like a
horse just shit in her handbag.

Billy Connolly

People expect me to neigh, grind
my teeth, paw the ground and swish
my tail – none of which is easy.

Princess Anne

There is no secret as close as
that between rider and horse.

R. S. Surtees

Few girls are so well shaped
as a good horse.

Christopher Morley

People on horses look better
than they really are.

Marya Mannes

I got a horse for
my wife. I thought
it was a fair swap.

Bob Monkhouse

GARDENS OF EDEN

What a man needs
in gardening is
a cast-iron back
with a hinge in it.

Charles Dudley Warner

There are three things beginning
with G that we should avoid in life:
golf, gardening and gonorrhoea.

Dom Joly

❦

We may think we're nurturing
our garden but of course it's our
garden that is really nurturing us.

Jenny Uglow

❦

To turn ordinary clothes
into gardening clothes,
simply mix with compost.

Guy Browning

Old gardeners don't die. They
just throw in the trowel.

Audrey Austin

———◆———

A gardener is a bloke
who calls a spade a spade
– until he falls over one.

George Coote

———◆———

I'm not a dirt gardener. I sit
with my walking stick and point
things out that need to be done.
After many years the garden
is now totally obedient.

Sir Edwin Hardy Amies

Though an old man, I am
but a young gardener.

Thomas Jefferson

Did you see the pictures of
the moon? They must have
the same gardener I have.

Harry Hershfield

If you think 'Hoe hoe' is a laughing
matter, you're no gardener.

Herbert Prochnow

A man of words and not of deeds
Is like a garden full of weeds.

Proverb

A garden is a thing of
beauty and a job forever.

Barry Tobin

I have nothing against
gardening. I just prefer not to
be there when it happens.

Tracy McLeod

Nothing grows in our
garden, only washing.

Dylan Thomas

Nature soon takes over if
the gardener is absent.

Penelope Hobhouse

Many things grow in the garden
that were never sown there.

Thomas Fuller

A garden is but nature debauched.

Henry David Thoreau

❖

Don't wear perfume in the garden unless you want to be pollinated by bees.

Anne Raver

❖

To lock horns with nature, the only equipment you really need is the constitution of Paul Bunyan and the basic training of a commando.

S. J. Perelman

Gardening requires lots of water -
most of it in the form of perspiration.

Lou Erickson

A man should never plant a garden
larger than his wife can take care of.

T. H. Everett

NATURE'S LARDER

A cauliflower is
a cabbage with a
college education.

Mark Twain

Tomatoes and squash never fail
to reach maturity. You can spray
them with acid, beat them with
sticks and burn them; they love it.

S. J. Perelman

❧

As to the garden, it seems to
me its chief fruit is blackbirds.

William Morris

❧

I want death to find me
planting my cabbages.

Michael de Montaigne

Cabbage. A familiar garden
vegetable about as large and
wise as a man's head.

Ambrose Bierce

Vegetables are interesting
but lack a sense of purpose
when unaccompanied by
a good cut of meat.

Fran Lebowitz

I do not like broccoli. And I haven't
liked it since I was a little kid
and my mother made me eat it. And
I'm President of the United
States and I'm not going to
eat any more broccoli.

George W. Bush

'Would you like
some manure for
your rhubarb?'
'No, we always have
ice cream on ours.'

Brendan Grace

Strawberries are the
angels of the earth,
innocent and sweet
with green leafy wings
reaching heavenward.

Jasmine Heiler

BORN IN A BARN

The moon is brighter
since the barn burned.

Matsuo Basho

I've been taking batting practice
in my barn where nobody can
see me, so I may be better
than anyone thinks.

Garth Brooks

I was so naive as a kid I used to sneak
behind the barn and do nothing.

Johnny Carson

Do not let a flattering woman
coax and wheedle you and deceive
you; she is after your barn.

Hesiod

Any jackass can kick down
a barn but it takes a good
carpenter to build one.

Lyndon B. Johnson

If a farmer fills his barn with
grain, he gets mice. If he leaves
it empty, he gets actors.

Walter Scott

GETTING UPPITY

None of us have
our curtains made
by people who
haven't got a title.

Anne Robinson on living in Gloucestershire

It is an important general rule to
always refer to your friend's country
establishment as a 'cottage'.

Stephen Potter

An aristocrat is a democrat
gone to seed.

Ralph Emerson

A gentleman farmer
raises nothing
but his hat.

Don Bale

Not many of our
families can boast
that a Savile Row
tailor calls four times
a year at their country
estate to measure the
scarecrows in their
fields for new suits.

J. B. Morton

I have invented an
invaluable permanent
invalid called Bunbury
in order that I may
be able to go down
into the country
whenever I choose.

Oscar Wilde, *The Importance of Being Earnest*

A gentleman farmer
is one who tips his
hat every time he
passes a tomato.

Leopold Fechtner

Country manners dictate that
even if someone phones you up
to tell you your house is on fire,
first they ask how you are.

Alice Munro

There are just two classes in
good society in England: the
equestrian and the neurotic.

George Bernard Shaw

FEELING SHEEPISH

Bonnie Prince Charlie was the only man ever to be named after three sheepdogs.

Jonathan Ross

Red sky in the morning, shepherds
take warning. Red sky at night
– the bloody barn's on fire.

Jo Sherard

Mary had a little lamb.
The midwife fainted.

Leonard Rossiter

You have to have a good yarn to pull
the wool over a sheep farmer's eyes.

Noel V. Ginnity

And now here are
the results of the
Sheepdog Trials.
All the sheepdogs
were found not guilty.

Keith Waterhouse

They told me it takes three sheep to make a cardigan. I didn't even know they could knit.

Sue Gingold

A HUNTING WE
WILL GO

The English
country gentleman
galloping after a fox
– the unspeakable
in full pursuit of
the uneatable.

Oscar Wilde

I'm weary of the endless kerfuffle over fox hunting. I'm told there's a technical term for my condition: tallyhosis.

P. D. Clarke

A fox should not be on the jury at a goose's trial.

Thomas Fuller

I'm a hunt saboteur. I go out the night before and shoot the fox.

Peter Kay

Eat British Lamb: 50,000
Foxes Can't Be Wrong

Placard from the Countryside March, 1998

Unlike my predecessors I
have devoted more of my life
to shunting and hooting than
to hunting and shooting.

Sir Frederick Burrows

The fascination of shooting as
a sport depends almost wholly
on whether you are at the right
or wrong end of the gun.

P. G. Wodehouse

Men hunt because they have
something wrong with their
own equipment and need
something else to shoot.

Pamela Anderson

I'm getting to the age where I can only
enjoy the last sport left. It is called
'Hunting for your spectacles.'

Sir Edward Grey

SAY IT WITH FLOWERS

I was flattered to have a rose named after me until I read the description in the catalogue: No good in a bed, but perfect up against a wall.

Eleanor Roosevelt

I used to wear a flower in
my lapel, but the pot kept
bumping off my stomach.

Benny Hill

—◆—

I'd like to buy a bunch of
flowers for the woman I love,
but my wife won't let me.

Henny Youngman

—◆—

Children enjoy seeing flowers
coming up – by the roots.

Erma Bombeck

A rose by any other name
would be just as expensive.

Lambert Jeffries

***

Flowers are one of the few things
we buy and then watch die without
asking for our money back.

George Carlin

***

The ability of dandelions
to tell the time is somewhat
exaggerated. The time always
turns out to be 37 o'clock.

Miles Kington

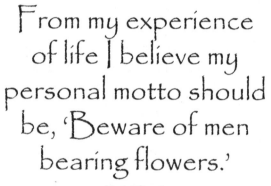

From my experience
of life I believe my
personal motto should
be, 'Beware of men
bearing flowers.'

Muriel Spark

UDDER MATTERS

To err is human,
to moo bovine.

Gwen Inglis

My wife's father said, 'If you marry my daughter I'll give you three acres and a cow.' I'm still waiting for the three acres.

Max Miller

———•———

Nature is amazing. Who would have thought of growing a fly swatter on the rear end of a cow?

Hal Roach

———•———

You can argue about foot and mouth until the cows come home.

Elliot Morley

I'm not saying my wife isn't a
nice person, but if she was living
in India she'd be sacred.

Les Dawson

Do you know why cream is so
much more expensive than milk?
Because the cows hate to
squat on those little bottles.

Kurt Vonnegut

Considering high fat milk is
bad for you, why don't more
cows get heart attacks?

Mort Sahl

Farmer from the dales to a friend:
'Nature is wonderful. Look at
the way she puts cream at the top
of milk so people can get it.'

Peg Bracken

—◦—

'Tell me, Kieran, how long
cows should be milked?'
'The same as short ones, sir.'

Tony Butler

I often wonder what the first person
who discovered how to milk a cow
was at when he discovered it!

Pat Ingoldsby

His farm is so small, the cows
only give condensed milk.

Leopold Fechtner

The best way to stop milk from
turning sour is to leave it in the cow.

Kevin Goldstein-Jackson

Old dairy farmers never die.
They just go out to pasture.

Audrey Austin

It was so hot the cows were
giving evaporated milk.

Groucho Marx

There's no use crying over spilt milk.
It only makes it harder to clean up.

Woody Allen

GREEN GREEN
GRASS OF HOME

The grass is always
greener over the
septic tank.

Erma Bombeck

The kind of grass I've got in the garden lies down under the mower and pops up again as soon as it's passed.

Basil Boothroyd

If the grass is greener in the
other fellow's garden, let him
worry about mowing it.

Paddy Murray

If the grass is greener in the
other fellow's garden, let him
worry about mowing it.

Parks are but pavements disguised
with a growth of grass.

George Gissing

A lawn is nature under
totalitarian rule.

Michael Pollan

Nothing is more pleasant to the eye
than green grass kept finely shorn.

Francis Bacon

Grass is hard and lumpy and damp,
and full of dreadful black insects.

Oscar Wilde

THE BIRDS AND
THE BEES

I've got enough
crows' feet to start
a bird sanctuary.

Kathy Lette

It isn't so much how busy you are
but why you're busy. The bee is
praised but the mosquito is swatted.

Roger Devlin

———•———

The early bird usually wishes he'd
let someone else get up first.

Elliott Gould

———•———

The late bird gets the worm because
the early one is knackered.

Graham Hogarth

A bird in the hand... invariably does something nasty on your wrist.

Anonymous

A bird in the hand is useless when you have to blow your nose.

Henny Youngman

The early bird gets the late one's breakfast.

Guy Pepper

Why did the bees go on strike?
For shorter flowers and more honey.

Brian Johnston

My wife does bird imitations.
She watches me like a hawk.

Milton Berle

A bird in the hand is
bad table manners.

L. L. Levinson

Imagine if birds were tickled by
feathers. You'd see a flock of them
coming by laughing hysterically.

Steven Wright

It's hard to kill two birds
if one is stoned.

Brush Shiels

A bird in the hand is usually dead.

Jeff Wilson

The early bird gets
the worm. The early
worm gets eaten.

Norman Augustine

BACK TO NATURE

Great things are
done when men and
mountains meet.
This is not done by
jostling in the street.

William Blake

Remote: a place with only
one big modern hotel.

J. B. Morton

The greatest joy in nature
is the absence of man.

Bliss Carman

If you take the path less travelled,
maybe it's because you march
to the beat of a different drum.
On the other hand, maybe
you're just completely lost.

Patrick Murray

My living in Yorkshire
was so far out of the
way that it was actually
12 miles from a lemon.

Sydney Smith

I like long walks, especially
when they're taken by
people who annoy me.

Fred Allen

Marry an outdoor woman. Then
if you throw her out in the yard
for the night she can still survive.

W. C. Fields

A location where, it can
be argued, there are never
enough comfortable chairs.

Fran Lebowitz on nature

Thank heavens the sun has
gone in and I don't have to
go out and enjoy it.

Logan Pearsall Smith

One thing is certain about
going outdoors. When you come
back in, you'll be scratching.

P. J. O'Rourke

Camping: nature's way of
promoting the motel industry.

Dave Barry, *Dave Barry's Only Travel
Guide You'll Ever Need*

My landlady told me
to put on a new pair of
socks every day. By
Saturday I couldn't
get my wellies on.

Kevin McAleer on hiking

Fieldes have eies and
woods have eares.

John Heywood

HOGWASH

I have been sticking up for you. Someone said you weren't fit to live with pigs and I said you were.

Lord Berners to an acquaintance

I was worried about the smell but
it didn't prove to be a problem.
After a while he got used to it.

Quentin Crisp on having a pet pig

Why do we wait until a pig
is dead to cure it?

Danny Cummins

A slice of ham is better than
a fat pig in a dream.

Proverb

All dogs look up to you. All cats look down on you. Only a pig looks at you as an equal.

Winston Churchill

What would happen to the economy if pigs could fly? Bacon would go up.

Brian Johnston

I'd rather kiss my pigs than my husband.

Sue Parkinson

If you covered a sow's ear with silk
purses, the damn bristles would
still work their way through.

Marie Lloyd

What's the main difference
between men and pigs? Pigs don't
get drunk and act like men.

Cynthia Heimel

I'm very fond of pigs;
but I don't find it
hard to eat them.

Robert Runcie

EGGS-CITING TIMES

Last year I crossed
a parrot with a hen.
When it lays an egg
now, it comes over
and tells me about it.

Merrit Malloy

Then there was a farmer who got rid of his incubator because he'd had it over six months and it hadn't laid even one egg.

Doug Sanderson

———◆———

Noise proves nothing. Often a hen who has merely laid an egg cackles as if she had laid an asteroid.

Mark Twain

———◆———

It was so windy last week our hen laid the same egg three times.

Des MacHale

An optimistic farmer in the
West Country gave hot water
to his hens because he wanted
them to lay boiled eggs.

Lambert Jeffries

I see that eggs are going up
again. God help the chickens.

Maureen Potter

Don't put all your eggs
in one bastard.

Dorothy Parker

Which came first, the
chicken or the egg?
Or was it the rooster?

Jackie Mason

THIS LAND IS
YOUR LAND

I am not the type who
wants to go back
to the land. I am the
type who wants to go
back to the hotel.

Fran Lebowitz

It will be said of this generation that it found England a land of beauty and left it a land of beauty spots.

C. E. M. Joad

An acre of Middlesex is better than a principality in Utopia.

Lord Macaulay

My father always said, 'Own the land you live on. Then you can piss on it without being arrested.'

Richard Harris

Land is the only thing that lasts in life. Money burns like tinder. And as for government promises, the wind is steadier.

Louise Erdrich

It is a comfortable feeling to know that you can stand on your own ground. Land is about the only thing that can't fly away.

Anthony Trollope

It gives one position and prevents one from keeping it up. That is all that can be said about land.

Oscar Wilde

When I go out into
the countryside and
see the sun and the
green and everything
flowering, I say to
myself, 'yes indeed, all
that belongs to me!'

Henri Rousseau

IT'S A DOG'S LIFE

If a dog jumps onto your lap it's because he's fond of you. If a cat does it it's because your lap is warm.

A. N. Whitehead

I taught my dog to beg. Last night he came home with £8.

Rodney Dangerfield

I poured spot remover on my dog. Now he's gone.

Steven Wright

Sign in a vet's office: 'Back in Ten Minutes. Sit!'

Joe McNamara

Women who can't bear to be
separated from their pet dogs
often send their children to
boarding schools quite cheerfully.

George Bernard Shaw

Pavlov taught the dog to eat
when he heard a bell. Two weeks
later he savaged the postman.

Bob Monkhouse

Personally I don't see why a
man can't have a dog and a
girl. But if you can only afford
one of them, get a dog.

Groucho Marx

Dogs laugh with their tails.

Max Eastman

It's dog eat dog in this rat race.

John Deacon

I sent my dog to obedience
school. He still bites me, but
now he says grace first.

Henny Youngman

Don't make the mistake of treating your dogs like human beings or they'll treat you like dogs.

Martha Scott

My dog's just like one of the
family. I won't say which one.

Bob Hope

We had to get rid of the kids. One
of the dogs was allergic to them.

Annie Lewis

I've got a miniature poodle.
The miniature about to
turn, it does a poodle.

Jackie Gleason

My dog is so lazy he doesn't chase
cars. He just sits on the kerb taking
down licence plate numbers.

Rodney Dangerfield

The great pleasure of a dog is that you may make a fool of yourself with him and not only will he not scold you, but he will make a fool of himself too.

Samuel Butler

If you eliminate smoking and gambling, you will be amazed to find that almost all an Englishman's pleasures can be, and mostly are, shared by his dog.

George Bernard Shaw

A dog is not
intelligent. Never
trust an animal
that is surprised
by his own farts.

Frank Skinner

DOWN TO EARTH

If you water it and it dies, it's a plant. If you pull it out and it grows back, it's a weed.

Gerry Daly

I like to tease my plants. I
water them with ice cubes.

Steven Wright

———•———

What is a weed? A plant whose
virtues have not yet been discovered.

Ralph Waldo Emerson

———•———

I don't have a green thumb. I
can't even get mould to grow
on last month's takeaway.

Johnny Gibson

'I might have ploughed that one myself,' said his father admiringly, 'if I'd been blindfolded and short of one arm, and with a team of horses that rocketed about like steeplechasers.'

A. G. Macdonell, *England, Their England*

Beware makers of crop circles. They're cereal killers.

Milton Berle

Every man reaps what he sows in this life – except the amateur gardener.

Lesley Hall

A bachelor flat is where all the
house plants are dead but there's
something growing in the refrigerator.

Marshall Williams

I don't exactly have a green
thumb. I once killed a flagpole.

Milton Berle

RURAL RIDDLES

He asked me if I'd
lived all my life in
the country. I said,
'I don't know. I'm
not dead yet.'

Sid Sugden

Why do cows have bells?
Because their horns don't work.

Janet Rogers

The farmer sows the seed. The
farmer's wife sews the clothes.
So how do you spell what the
farmer and his wife both do?

Martin Holleran

If owls are so wise, why don't
they get off the night shift?

Louis Safian

Would a laughing stock be a set
of cattle with a sense of humour?

Jack Cruise

—◆—

Teacher: Who was unhappy at
the return of the Prodigal Son?
Pupil: The fatted calf, sir.

Paddy Crosbie

—◆—

I used to know a bloke who
thought a kipper was a fish
that slept most of the time.

Tony Hancock

Did you hear about the rural magician? He was able to turn his tractor into a field.

Donal McDermott

If a cow laughed, would milk come out of her nose?

Paul O'Grady

Is a dogma the mother of pups?

Peter Eldin

If a pig loses its voice,
is it disgruntled?

Huw Jarsz

Did you hear about the man
who stayed up all night to
see where the sun went?
In the morning it dawned on him.

Jack Cruise

What do gardeners do when they retire?

Bob Monkhouse

Why did the hedgehog
cross the road?
To find his flat mate.

Nancy Sheridan

If we aren't supposed to eat animals,
why are they made of meat?

Jo Brand

Do goats date seriously or
are they only kidding?

Colin Keough

How is it one careless match can start a forest fire, but it takes a whole box to start a campfire?

Huw Jarsz

THE IMPORTANCE
OF BEING IDLE

If you're in the
country, take nothing
but pictures, leave
nothing but footprints,
kill nothing but time.

Hunter Davies

In the country, every day
is like Sunday.

John Waters

———◆———

The country is a place
where you have nothing to
do, and all day to do it.

John D. Sheridan

———◆———

When I am in the country I wish
to vegetate like the country.

William Hazlitt, *Table Talk*

Even if a farmer
intends to loaf, he
gets up early to start.

Edgar Watson Howe

I like to go fishing because it
gives me something to do while
I'm not doing anything.

Jack Charlton

Country life is pure and
unadulterated. They get up early
because they have so much to do
and go to bed early because they
have so little to think about.

Oscar Wilde

FISH OUT OF WATER

Old fishermen
don't die. They just
smell that way.

Audrey Austin

There are more fish taken out
of a stream than were ever in it.

Oliver Herford

There are more fish taken out

Fishing, with me, has always been
an excuse to drink in the daytime.

Jimmy Cannon

There's a fine line between
fishing and standing on the
shore looking like an idiot.

Steven Wright

Catch a man a fish and you can sell it to him. Teach a man to fish and you ruin a wonderful business opportunity.

Karl Marx

Fly-fishing is the most fun you can have standing up.

Arnold Gingrich

Have you heard about the oyster that went to the disco and pulled a mussel?

Billy Connolly

The trouble with
fish is that they go
on their holidays
around the same
time as fishermen.

Sid Caesar

I was often tempted to give up fishing and take up something less stressful – like alligator wrestling.

George Melly

Fishing is unquestionably a form of madness. But happily, for the once bitten there is no cure.

Sir Alec Douglas-Home

Fishing is a delusion entirely surrounded by liars in old clothes.

Don Marquis

On fishing shows they always throw
the fish back. They just want to
make them late for something.

Mitch Hedberg

———

Men and fish are alike. They
both get into trouble when
they open their mouths.

Jimmy Moore

———

A fishing rod is a stick with a worm
at one end and a fool at the other.

Samuel Johnson

It is to be observed that 'angling'
is the name given to fishing
by people who can't fish.

Stephen Leacock

———•———

All you need to be a fisherman
is patience and a worm.

Herb Shriner

———•———

How far a fisherman will
stretch the truth depends
on the length of his arms.

Thomas Jefferson

May the holes in your net be
no larger than the fish in it.

An Irish blessing

The fishing was good; it was
the catching that was bad.

A. K. Best

No human being, however great or
powerful, was ever as free as a fish.

John Ruskin

ALL CREATURES
GREAT AND SMALL

Animals generally
return the love
you lavish on them
by a swift bite in
passing – not unlike
friends and wives.

Gerald Durrell

Whenever you observe an animal
closely, you feel as if a human being
is sitting inside making fun of you.

Elias Canetti

Animals are such agreeable
friends. They ask no questions,
pass on no criticisms.

George Eliot

A rabbit's foot may be lucky
– but not for the original owner.

Fred Metcalf

It's obvious that carrots are good for your eyesight. Have you ever seen a rabbit wearing glasses?

Steve McQueen

If music is the food of love,
why don't rabbits sing?

D. J. Hurst

Our donkey isn't a pet. We
just have it for kicks.

Don Rickles

Animal testing is totally unfair.
They all get nervous and
give the wrong answers.

Stephen Fry

A hootenanny is a cross
between an owl and a goat.

John Crosbie

In the world of mules
there are no rules.

Ogden Nash

I don't mind an animal sharing my
bed, but I strongly object to being
woken at five o'clock in the morning
by an enthusiastic squirrel trying
to push a peanut in my ear.

Gerald Durrell

MAD AS A MARCH HARE

Before you let
the sun in, mind it
wipes its shoes.

Dylan Thomas

You don't see many red squirrels
since they became extinct.

Michael Aspel

All animals are equal, but some
are more equal than others.

George Orwell, *Animal Farm*

We find the man who stole
the horse not guilty.

Alleged verdict of rural jury in Pembrokeshire

When I talk to plants
they respond to me.

Prince Charles

Last year I went
fishing with Salvador
Dali. He was using a
dotted line. He caught
every other fish.

Steven Wright

NICE WEATHER
FOR DUCKS

My favourite
British weather
forecast, culled from
a newspaper reads:
'Dry and warm, but
cooler with some rain.'

Bill Bryson

Rain is one thing the British do
better than anybody else.

Marilyn French

Rain is one thing the British do

If you want the rainbow you
gotta put up with the rain.

Dolly Parton

Rain is something that, when you
take an umbrella, it doesn't.

Herbert Prochnow

Why don't sheep shrink
when it rains?

Steven Wright

———◆———

Rain makes flowers grow
– and taxis disappear.

Hal Roach

———◆———

In Cornwall I overheard the
following: 'You can tell it's
summer. The rain is warmer.'

Mervyn Madge

Rain will travel for thousands of miles against the prevailing winds for the opportunity to rain on a tent.

Dave Barry

We could all take a lesson from the weather. It pays no attention to criticism.

Mary Kennedy

If God had intended man to live in England, he'd have given him gills.

David Renwick

There is really no
such thing as bad
weather, only different
kinds of good weather.

Lord Avebury

THE HUMAN ANIMAL

The more I see
of men, the more
I admire dogs.

Brigitte Bardot

Man is the only animal that
can remain on friendly terms
with the victims he intends
to eat until he eats them.

Samuel Butler

Man is the only animal that
blushes – or needs to.

Mark Twain

Human beings were invented by
water as a device for transporting
itself from one place to another.

Tom Robbins

The male is a kind
of domestic animal
which, if treated with
firmness and kindness,
can be trained to
do most things.

Jilly Cooper

Men! The only animal
in the world to fear.

D. H. Lawrence

SEASONAL HUMOUR

Spring is the
time of year when
fishermen begin to
get that faraway
lake in their eyes.

Herbert Prochnow

It's spring in England. I missed it last year. I was in the bathroom.

Michael Flanders

Now is the winter of our discontent made glorious summer by central heating.

Jack Sharkey

Hurrah! It is a frost – the dahlias are dead.

R. S. Surtees

One of the most pleasing sounds
of springtime, to be heard all over
the country, is the contented
cooing of osteopaths as Man
picks up his garden spade.

Oliver Pritchett

Now is the time of year when
the bulbs you forgot to plant
last autumn will fail to bloom.

George Coote

If Mother Nature wanted autumn
to be really beautiful, she would
have raked up the leaves herself.

Gene Perret

I hate allergy season.
It's Mother Nature's
way of telling me
flowers get more
sex than I do.

Basil White

Summer has set in with
its usual severity.

Samuel Taylor Coleridge

Every autumn the world of nature
turns brown, red and yellow – just
like the decayed food in my fridge.

Bob Monkhouse

Leaves are verbs that
conjugate the seasons.

Gretel Ehrlich

There's one good
thing about snow,
it makes your lawn
look as nice as
your neighbour's.

Clyde Moore

VILLAGE LIFE

When you left home,
you deprived the
village of its idiot.

Anonymous

Few things are more pleasant
than a good village graced
with a good church, a good
priest and a good pub.

John Hillaby

A village is a hive of glass, where
nothing unobserved can pass.

Charles H. Spurgeon

To know after absence the
familiar street and road and
village and house is to know
again the satisfaction of home.

Hal Borland

If you would be
known, and not know,
vegetate in a village;
if you would know,
and not be known,
live in the city.

Charles Caleb Colton

WOOD YOU BELIEVE IT

The sky is held
up by the trees.

Native American saying

Every tree has its own place upon
this earth. Only man has lost his way.

Margaret Craven

There was once a tree surgeon
who had a nasty accident.
He fell out of his patient.

Tommy Cooper

Trees are much like human beings
and enjoy each other's company.
Only a few love to be alone.

Jens Jensen

Great trees are good for
nothing but shade.

George Herbert

For sale: bonsai tree. Large.

Jimmy Carr

'Every day my dog and I go
for a tramp in the woods.'
'Does the dog enjoy it?'
'Yes, but the tramp's
getting a bit fed up.'

Nigel Rees

Plant trees – they
give us two of the
most crucial elements
for survival: oxygen
and books.

Whitney Brown

Trees display the
effects of breeding
quite as much as
horses, dogs or men.

William Howitt

GETTING AWAY
FROM IT ALL

I've finally realised
what I don't like
about holidays in
the country. My
wife comes with me.

Les Dawson

I'm not wild about holidays.
They always seem a ludicrously
expensive way of proving
there's no place like home.

Jilly Cooper

❦

'Capable widow, no
sense of humour, some
knowledge of haemorrhoids
preferred.' Not a reply.

Victoria Wood on advertising for a holiday companion

The man who said, 'You can't take it with you' never saw my family pack for a holiday.

Hal Roach

People go on holidays to get away from it all, and then open their bags to find they've brought it all with them.

Maureen Potter

A DAY AT THE RACES

Horses have four
bits of luck nailed
to their feet. They
should be the luckiest
animals in the world.

Eddie Izzard

I never kept racehorses.
They kept me.

Horatio Bottomley

—◦—

The last horse I backed came in so
late, the jockey was wearing pyjamas.

Joe E. Lewis

—◦—

A horse show is a lot of horses
showing their asses to a lot of
horses' asses showing their horses.

Denis Leary

A racehorse is the only animal
that can take thousands of people
for a ride at the same time.

Herbert Prochnow

The last horse I backed was so
slow, the jockey died of starvation.

Milton Berle

The great thing about racehorses is that you don't need to take them for walks.

Albert Finney

The best way to stop a runaway horse is to bet on him.

Jeffrey Bernard

Horse sense is a good judgement which keeps horses from betting on people.

W. C. Fields

TRAVELS WITH MY ANT

If ants are such busy
workers, how come
they find time to go
to all the picnics?

Marie Dressler

The problem with picnics is that
they're always held on a holiday
– when the ants have the day off too.

Gene Perret

The ideal holiday resort is where
the fish bite but the insects don't.

John D. Sheridan

Ants are insects
that attend picnics
for a living.

Kenny Everett

The ideal place for
a picnic is usually a
little further on.

Robert Morley

COUNTRY LIFE:
THE CASE FOR

You can be a little
ungrammatical if you
come from the right
part of the country.

Robert Frost

The country is the only place
where they have night left.

Ursula LeGuin

⊷•⊶

The city is not a concrete
jungle. It is a human zoo.

Desmond Morris

⊷•⊶

We do not look in great cities
for our best morality.

Jane Austen

God made the country, and
man made the town.

William Cowper, *The Task*

The modern city is a place
for banking and prostitution,
and very little else.

Frank Lloyd Wright

I lived in solitude in the country and
noticed how the monotony of a quiet
life stimulates the creative mind.

Albert Einstein

Nature never makes any
blunders. When she does
something foolish she means it.

Josh Billings

❦

Farmers worry only during
the growing season, but town
people worry all the time.

Edgar Watson Howe

❦

The pleasure of a country life lies
in the eternally renewed evidences
of the determination to live.

Vita Sackville-West

It is only in the country that we can get to know a person or a book.

Cyril Connolly

—◆—

When one is in the town one amuses oneself. When one is in the country one amuses other people.

Oscar Wilde

COUNTRY LIFE: THE CASE AGAINST

Country life isn't
so much tiptoeing
through the tulips
as slip-slopping
through the cow shit.

Kenny Everett

The fairest thing in nature, a
flower, still has its roots in manure.

D. H. Lawrence

The lowest and vilest alleys in
London do not present a more
dreadful record of sin than does the
smiling and beautiful countryside.

Sir Arthur Conan Doyle

Country life is fittest for
disgraced persons.

Lettice Knollys

Two pieces of advice
if you're going to the
country: first, look
out for number one.
And second, try not
to step in number two.

Paul Carmody

There is nothing good to be
had in the country. If there is,
they will not let you have it.

William Hazlitt

❧

Nothing ages like a woman
living in the country.

Colette

❧

The country is laid out in a
haphazard and sloppy fashion,
offensive to the tidy mind.

Alan Brien

I've just bought a fantastic house
in the country. It's just a half hour
from London – by phone.

Ted Cullen

I live in the country. It's so
boring we have bets on things
like whether we're going to
have weather tomorrow.

Marian Peel

It is a place with only one post a
day... In the country I always fear
creation will expire before tea-time.

Sydney Smith

Technology for
Country Folk
Floppy Disc: What
you get from carrying
too much wood.
Byte: What flies do
Modem: What you
did to the hay fields

Anonymous

Anybody can be
good in the country.
There are no
temptations there.

Oscar Wilde

www.summersdale.com